SANTOSH THORAT

Secrets To Beat Constipation

Copyright © 2023 by Santosh Thorat

All rights reserved. No part of this publication may be reproduced, stored or transmitted in any form or by any means, electronic, mechanical, photocopying, recording, scanning, or otherwise without written permission from the publisher. It is illegal to copy this book, post it to a website, or distribute it by any other means without permission.

First edition

This book was professionally typeset on Reedsy.
Find out more at reedsy.com

Secrets
To
Beat
Constipation

by Ancient Ways

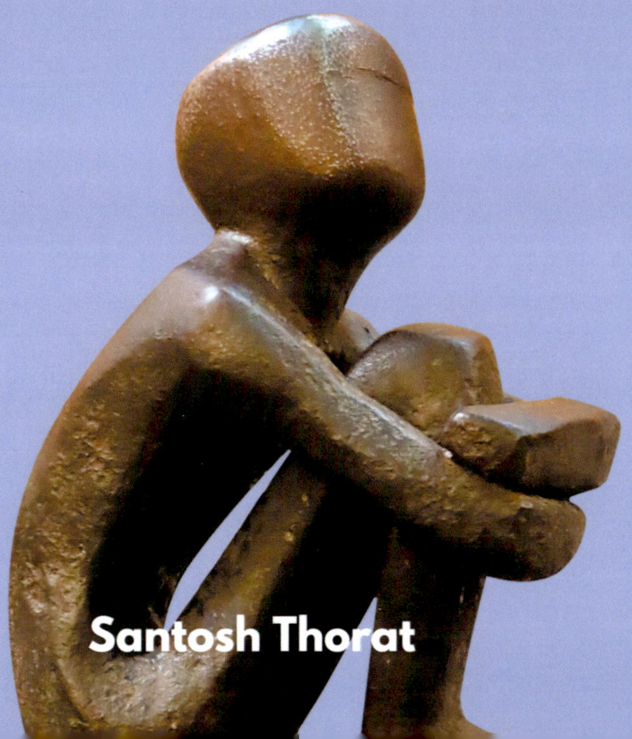

Santosh Thorat

Contents

1

My Words

I am truly thankful to Shivshakti and my all Gurus for Divine Blessings

Step into the world of ancient wisdom, with a profound focus on digestive health. With years of dedicated exploration and a commitment to understanding the body's intricate balance, We brought you "Secrets To beat Constipation by Ancient Ways"

This book is not just a guide; it's a voyage through time, where ancient techniques meet contemporary challenges. We carefully weaved together the wisdom of our ancestors with the latest insights into digestive health, creating a tapestry of knowledge that holds the key to relieving constipation naturally.

As you flip through the pages, you'll encounter a wealth of knowledge that empowers you to take charge of your well-being. Whether you're seeking immediate relief or aiming for long-term gut health, this book provides a roadmap enriched with time-tested remedies.

Immerse yourself in the synergy of ancient practices and modern understanding, guided by ancient expertise. 'Secrets To beat Constipation by Ancient Ways' is not just a book; it's a transformative journey toward a more balanced and harmonious life. Your journey to relief and wellness begins here.

2

Reasons Behind Constipation

In today's fast-paced world, constipation has become an unwelcome companion for many. The culprits behind this common woe are often rooted in our modern lifestyle.

Firstly, our sedentary habits play a starring role. With the rise of desk jobs and screen time, physical activity takes a backseat. The lack of movement slows down the digestive system, making it harder for food to journey through our bodies smoothly.

Processed foods add another layer to the constipation puzzle. Our diets, often laden with refined sugars and low fiber content, contribute to sluggish digestion. Fiber, a hero in promoting bowel regularity, is often sidelined in favor of convenient but less nutritious options.

Hydration, or rather the lack of it, is another suspect. In the hustle and bustle, many of us forget to drink enough water. Dehydration can turn stool dry and hard, leading to difficulty in passing it.

Stress, a constant companion in our fast-paced lives, also raises its hand. The mind-gut connection is powerful, and stress can throw our digestive system off balance, slowing down the natural rhythm of bowel movements.

Lastly, ignoring the call of nature becomes a common practice. Our busy schedules sometimes push us to postpone bathroom breaks, disrupting the body's natural signals and contributing to constipation.

In essence, modern constipation often stems from a combination of insufficient physical activity, poor dietary choices, inadequate hydration, heightened stress levels, and neglecting the body's natural cues. Addressing these aspects can be the key to bidding farewell to the discomfort of constipation and embracing a healthier, more balanced lifestyle.

"A Healthy Gut Empowers Healthy Body "

3

Ancient Remedies for Constipation

Hot Glass of Water with Yoga:

Starting your day with a simple routine can have profound effects on your overall well-being. One easy and beneficial practice is to begin your morning with a slightly hot glass of water. This uncomplicated step can set a positive tone for the day ahead, helping to kickstart your metabolism and promote hydration.

Drinking water in the morning has several health benefits. Overnight, your body goes without water for an extended period, and rehydrating in the morning is a gentle way to replenish fluids. Opting for a slightly hot glass can be soothing to your digestive system, aiding in the elimination of toxins and promoting a healthy gut.

Now, imagine complementing this hydration ritual with a brief yoga session. You don't need to be an expert yogi to reap the rewards; a mere 5 to 10 minutes of simple morning yoga (as shown in picture) can make a significant difference.

By incorporating this short yoga routine into your morning, you're not only awakening your body but also setting a positive tone for the day. These simple poses promote flexibility, improve circulation, and enhance your overall sense of well-being. Remember, it's not about perfection but about cultivating a mindful and gentle start to your day. So, after that refreshing glass of slightly hot water, give your body the gift of movement and mindfulness. Your mornings will thank you, and you might just find yourself approaching each day with a renewed sense of energy and calm.

4

Daily Exercise with Kapalbhati

Regular exercise plays a crucial role in maintaining both physical and mental well-being. Among various exercises, incorporating Kapalbhati into your daily routine can be a game-changer for your health. Let's delve into the simplicity and effectiveness of this practice.

Why Exercise Matters:

Exercise is like a magic potion for our bodies. It keeps our heart healthy, boosts our mood, and strengthens our muscles. Engaging in physical activity regularly is a commitment to a healthier and happier life. Whether it's a brisk walk, a jog, or a workout routine, the benefits are countless.

Enter Kapalbhati:

Now, let's focus on a specific exercise known as Kapalbhati. It's a breathing technique rooted in ancient yoga practices. The name itself is derived from two Sanskrit words: 'Kapal,' meaning skull, and 'Bhati,' which translates to shining or illuminating. Essentially, Kapalbhati is a breath-cleansing exercise that not only rejuvenates your body but also brings a radiant glow to your face.

How to Do Kapalbhati:

The beauty of Kapalbhati lies in its simplicity. Find a quiet space, sit comfortably with your spine straight, and close your eyes. Take a deep breath in, and as you exhale, forcefully contract your abdominal muscles, pushing the air out in short bursts. Allow the inhalation to happen naturally without much effort. It's like a rhythmic pumping of the abdomen.

Now, the key is consistency. Start with 30 to 50 shots per day. As you get comfortable with the practice, you can gradually increase the count. The emphasis is not on the number but on maintaining the quality of each breath. Keep the pace steady and controlled.

5

The Magic Behind Kapalbhati

The Magic Behind Kapalbhati:

1. *Detoxification:*

Kapalbhati is renowned for its detoxifying effects. As you engage in this breathing exercise, you're not just expelling air; you're releasing toxins from your body. It's like giving your internal system a refreshing cleanse.

2. *Energizing the Body:*

The rapid exhalations in Kapalbhati increase the intake of oxygen, revitalizing your body and mind. This burst of energy can be a natural and invigorating start to your day.

3. *Stress Buster:*

The controlled and rhythmic nature of Kapalbhati triggers a relaxation response in your nervous system. It's a potent stress management tool that can be practiced by anyone, regardless of age or fitness level.

4. *Improves Digestion:*

The abdominal contractions in Kapalbhati massage and stimulate the digestive organs. This, in turn, enhances digestion and can be beneficial for those dealing with digestive issues.

6

Incorporating Kapalbhati into Your Daily Routine

aking Kapalbhati a part of your daily routine doesn't require a significant time commitment. You can seamlessly integrate it into your morning or evening schedule. Find a quiet corner, roll out a yoga mat if you prefer, and allocate just a few minutes to this practice.

The morning is an ideal time to kickstart your day with Kapalbhati. It not only wakes up your body but also primes your mind for the challenges ahead. If mornings are hectic, evenings work just as well. It can be a soothing way to unwind after a long day.

In the hustle and bustle of modern life, taking care of our well-being is often neglected. Exercise, especially in the form of a mindful practice like Kapalbhati, offers a holistic approach to health. It's not just about building muscles or losing weight; it's about nurturing your body and mind.

So, as you embark on this journey of daily exercise, consider the simplicity and effectiveness of Kapalbhati. In 30 to 50 shots a day, you have a powerful tool to enhance your overall well-being. Remember, it's not just about the quantity; it's about the mindful quality of each breath that can transform your health in a profound way.

(Avoid Kapalbhati in Pregnancy)

7

Ancient Mantras

In the quiet moments just before sleep, we find ourselves in a unique space—a threshold between the hustle and bustle of the day and the serenity of the night. It's in this tranquil interlude that a simple practice can weave its way into our routine, bringing about a sense of peace and well-being. The ancient art of chanting mantras silently in the mind before drifting into slumber can be a powerful ritual for enhancing both mental and physical health.

Let's delve into a practice that involves the gentle repetition of sacred sounds, accompanied by prayers aimed at fostering a deep connection with the divine. The chosen mantras for this bedtime ritual are "**Nama Shivaya**" and "**Om Jum Saha**." These mantras, when embraced with sincerity and intention, can serve as gateways to a more profound sense of calm and vitality.

8

The Setting

Picture yourself in the quiet cocoon of your bedroom, the soft glow of moonlight filtering through the curtains. You've completed your evening routine and are now ready to surrender to the rejuvenating embrace of sleep. It's at this juncture that the practice unfolds.

Step 1: Prepare the Mind

Sit or lie down comfortably, taking a few moments to settle into a relaxed state. Close your eyes and breathe deeply, allowing the rhythm of your breath to naturally slow down. Let go of the day's worries and concerns. This is your time for tranquility.

Step 2: Choosing Your Mantra

Select either **_"Nama Shivaya"_** or **_"Om Jum Saha"_** as your chosen mantra for the night. Each holds its own vibrational energy and significance. "Nama Shivaya" invokes the divine presence of Lord Shiva, while "Om Jum Saha" is a mantra associated with universal energy and well-being.

Step 3: Silent Chanting

Begin the silent chanting of your chosen mantra. As you breathe in and out, let the sacred syllables resonate within your mind. Visualize the sound waves creating a cocoon of positive energy around you. The repetition should be gentle, a rhythmic hum that aligns with the natural cadence of your breath.

Step 4: Prayer Before Chanting

Before delving into the mantra, offer a heartfelt prayer. It could be as simple as expressing gratitude for the day's blessings and seeking divine protection for the night ahead. The prayer sets the tone for your practice, infusing it with a sense of reverence and purpose.

Step 5: Chanting in the Mind

As you continue chanting the mantra, allow your mind to gradually unwind. If distracting thoughts arise, gently guide your focus back to the mantra. The aim is not perfection but a sincere engagement with the sacred sounds.

Step 6: Prayer After Chanting

Conclude your mantra practice with another prayer, expressing gratitude for the healing and transformative power of the mantras. Envision the energy cultivated during this practice enveloping your body and mind, creating a shield of positivity and well-being.

Closing Thoughts:

This bedtime ritual, rooted in ancient wisdom, invites you to harness the power of sound and intention for holistic well-being. By incorporating silent mantra chanting into your nightly routine, you create a sacred space where stress dissipates, and a sense of calm prevails. The accompanying prayers act as bridges between the earthly and the divine, amplifying the resonance of your intentions.

As you embrace this practice, remember that its potency lies in sincerity and consistency. Over time, you may find that the ritual not only enhances your sleep quality but also permeates your waking hours with a newfound sense of vitality. So, as you close your eyes and embark on this journey of nocturnal serenity, may the whispered mantras pave the way for a restful and rejuvenating night's sleep—body, mind, and spirit harmonizing in the gentle embrace of the sacred sounds.

9

Changing Eating Habits

In the hustle and bustle of our daily lives, it's easy to overlook the impact of our eating habits on our overall well-being. One simple yet powerful piece of advice that often gets overshadowed is the wisdom of eating only three meals a day. And, there's an extra nugget of health gold – make that evening meal a light one, ideally consumed between 6 pm to 8 pm.

Let's break it down in a way that's not only easy to understand but also easy to incorporate into our busy schedules.

10

Happy Eating Habits

1. The Magic Number: Three Meals a Day

Imagine your body as a well-oiled machine. For this machine to function optimally, it needs fuel at regular intervals. Now, picture each meal as a pit stop where your body refuels and reenergizes. By limiting yourself to three main meals a day, you're allowing your digestive system to work efficiently, avoiding unnecessary strain.

Breakfast kickstarts your engine, lunch maintains the momentum, and dinner acts as the winding down phase. This approach prevents the constant snacking that can lead to overeating and weight gain. Moreover, it gives your digestive system some much-needed downtime between meals.

2. Lightening the Load: Evening Wisdom

As the day progresses, our energy needs naturally decrease. By adjusting our meal sizes accordingly, we align our eating habits with our body's natural rhythm. The key here is to keep the evening meal light, both in terms of portion size and the types of foods consumed.

A substantial dinner late in the evening can disrupt your sleep patterns and may lead to indigestion. Your body works hard during sleep to repair and rejuvenate, and it prefers not to be overloaded with the task of digesting a heavy meal. By opting for a lighter dinner, you're not only aiding your digestion but also promoting a more restful night's sleep.

3. The Golden Hours: 6 pm to 8 pm

Timing matters when it comes to meals. The period between 6 pm to 8 pm is considered ideal for dinner. During these hours, our body is still active, and digestion is more efficient. Eating within this timeframe allows your body to process the food before you hit the hay, contributing to a smoother and more effective digestion process.

It's like giving your digestive system a head start in the race against time, ensuring that by the time you tuck yourself into bed, your stomach isn't wrestling with a heavy load. This simple adjustment can make a world of difference in how you feel when you wake up the next morning.

11

Continuation

4. Practical Tips for Implementation

Making this shift in your eating habits doesn't have to be a daunting task. Here are some practical tips to ease into the rhythm:

Plan Your Meals:

Take a few minutes each week to plan your meals. This helps you ensure that you have nutritious options readily available and reduces the likelihood of reaching for unhealthy snacks.

Mindful Eating:

Pay attention to your body's hunger and fullness cues. Eat slowly and savor each bite. This not only aids digestion but also allows your brain to register when you're satisfied.

Hydration Matters:

Sometimes, our bodies confuse thirst with hunger. Stay hydrated throughout the day, and before reaching for a snack, consider whether you might just be in need of a glass of water.

Balanced Plate:

Aim for a well-balanced plate at each meal, incorporating a mix of proteins, carbohydrates, and healthy fats. This provides sustained energy and keeps you feeling satisfied longer.

In conclusion, the simple act of eating three meals a day, with a light dinner between 6 pm to 8 pm, can be a game-changer for your overall well-being. It's not about restrictive diets or counting calories; rather, it's about embracing a natural rhythm that aligns with your body's needs. By adopting this approach, you're not just eating to live; you're fueling your body in a way that supports a healthier and more balanced life.

Maintaining a healthy lifestyle is like embarking on a journey where your choices pave the way. One crucial aspect of this journey is managing what goes into your body. Let's explore three simple yet impactful guidelines that can make a significant difference: avoiding overeating, embracing the goodness of coconut water, and steering clear of the tempting world of junk food.

12

Continuation

1. The 70% Rule: Savor Every Bite

Imagine your stomach as a well-proportioned container, and your goal is to fill it just right. The 70% rule suggests that instead of indulging in a feast until you're bursting at the seams, it's wiser to stop when you feel about 70% full. This mindful approach not only prevents overeating but also allows your body to process food more efficiently.

When you slow down and savor each bite, you give your brain the time it needs to register the feeling of fullness. It's not about deprivation but rather about being in tune with your body's signals. Next time you sit down for a meal, pay attention to the flavors and textures. Put your fork down between bites, engage in conversation, and let your body communicate when it's satisfied.

2. Hydration Hero: Embrace Coconut Water

Staying adequately hydrated is a cornerstone of good health, and coconut water emerges as a refreshing hero in this quest. Packed with electrolytes, vitamins, and minerals, coconut water is a natural and delicious way to quench your thirst.

Swap sugary sodas and artificial energy drinks for the clear goodness of coconut water. Not only does it keep you hydrated, but it also provides a gentle energy boost without the unwanted calories and sugars found in many beverages. Whether you're hitting the gym or just navigating a busy day, make sipping on coconut water a daily habit.

Continuation

3. Junk the Junk: Bid Farewell to Unhealthy Temptations

In the modern world, the allure of fast food and snacks is undeniable. However, succumbing to these temptations often comes at the cost of your health. Junk food, laden with excess sugars, unhealthy fats, and artificial additives, can wreak havoc on your well-being.

Make a conscious effort to eliminate or at least minimize your consumption of junk food. Opt for wholesome, nutrient-rich alternatives like fruits, vegetables, and whole grains. When the urge for a snack strikes, reach for a handful of nuts, a piece of fruit, or a yogurt parfait. Your body will thank you for choosing fuel that nourishes rather than harms.

Embarking on a journey towards a healthier lifestyle doesn't have to be complicated. By incorporating these simple principles into your daily routine, you can create a foundation for long-term well-being. Remember the 70% rule to savor your meals, embrace the hydration hero that is coconut water, and bid farewell to the allure of junk food. Your body is a reflection of the choices you make, so choose wisely and savor the journey to a healthier you.

14

The Magic of Cow Ghee

1. Nutrient-Rich Goodness:

Cow ghee is a staple in traditional Indian cuisine and Ayurveda, appreciated not just for its rich flavor but also for its nutritional profile. It contains essential fatty acids, fat-soluble vitamins (A, E, and D), and antioxidants. These nutrients play a crucial role in promoting overall health, from supporting a robust immune system to maintaining healthy skin.

2. Improved Digestion:

Contrary to the misconception that all fats are detrimental, the saturated fats in cow ghee can aid in digestion. Ghee stimulates the secretion of stomach acids, helping to break down food more efficiently. It also supports a healthy gut lining, contributing to better absorption of nutrients.

3. Weight Management:

Incorporating cow ghee into your diet might seem counterintuitive for weight management, but moderate consumption can have positive effects. The healthy fats in ghee provide a sense of satiety, reducing overall calorie intake. Additionally, it contains medium-chain triglycerides (MCTs), which can be a source of energy for the body and may support weight loss efforts.

4. Lactose-Friendly:

Unlike butter, cow ghee is clarified, meaning the milk solids and impurities are removed. This process leaves behind the pure butterfat, making ghee an excellent option for those who are lactose intolerant. It provides the rich, buttery flavor without the digestive issues associated with lactose.

5. Stable at High Temperatures:

One remarkable quality of ghee is its high smoke point, which means it can withstand higher cooking temperatures without breaking down and forming harmful free radicals. This makes it a safe and healthier alternative for cooking methods like sautéing and frying.

15

Balancing Act with Fruit Juices

1. Antioxidant Boost:

Fruit juices, when consumed in moderation, offer a burst of essential vitamins, minerals, and antioxidants. These components help combat oxidative stress, which is linked to various chronic diseases and aging. Berries, citrus fruits, and pomegranates are particularly rich in antioxidants.

2. Hydration and Detoxification:

Staying hydrated is paramount for overall health, and fruit juices contribute to your daily fluid intake. Additionally, certain fruits possess natural detoxifying properties. For example, lemon juice is known for its ability to support liver function, aiding in the removal of toxins from the body.

3. Support for the Immune System:

The vitamin C content in many fruits, such as oranges and

kiwi, can give your immune system a significant boost. Regular intake of vitamin C is associated with a reduced risk of infections and can contribute to faster recovery from illnesses.

4. Natural Energy Source:

The natural sugars present in fruit juices provide a quick and accessible source of energy. This can be particularly beneficial before or after physical activity, offering a healthier alternative to artificially sweetened energy drinks.

5. Heart Health:

Some fruits, like grapes, are rich in polyphenols that support heart health. These compounds may help lower blood pressure, reduce inflammation, and improve overall cardiovascular function.

16

Balancing Your Plate

While cow ghee and fruit juices offer distinct health benefits, balance is key. Consider the following tips for a harmonious and nutritious diet:

1. Moderation is the Key:

Both cow ghee and fruit juices should be consumed in moderation. Excessive intake of ghee can contribute to an excess of calories, while too much fruit juice may lead to a surplus of natural sugars.

2. Diverse Diet:

Ensure your overall diet is diverse, incorporating a range of fruits, vegetables, whole grains, and lean proteins. This variety ensures you receive a broad spectrum of nutrients essential for optimal health.

3. Mindful Eating:

Pay attention to your body's signals of hunger and fullness. Mindful eating helps prevent overeating and encourages a healthy relationship with food.

4. Individualized Nutrition:

Dietary needs vary among individuals. Consider consulting with a nutritionist or healthcare professional to create a personalized plan that meets your unique requirements.

Incorporating cow ghee into your cooking and embracing the refreshing taste of fruit juices can be a delightful journey towards a healthier lifestyle. These choices, when made mindfully and in moderation, can contribute to overall well-being, providing your body with essential nutrients and supporting various aspects of health—from digestion to immunity. Remember, the key is balance and a diverse, nutrient-rich diet that caters to your individual needs and preferences.

17

The Hidden Wonders of Sleeping on Your Left Side: A Health Boost You Never Knew You Needed

I n the quest for a healthier lifestyle, we often focus on diet, exercise, and stress management. However, what if the secret to improved well-being lies in something as simple as the position you adopt while sleeping? It turns out that the way you position your body during sleep can have a significant impact on your health, and sleeping on your left side is emerging as a practice with a myriad of benefits.

The Basics of Sleep Position: More Than Just Comfort

Before delving into the advantages of sleeping on your left side, it's essential to understand that sleep position plays a crucial role in ensuring a good night's rest. People typically sleep in various positions—on their back, stomach, right side, or left side. Each position has its unique effects on the body, influencing everything from digestion to respiratory function.

The Left-Side Advantage for Digestive Harmony

One of the most notable benefits of sleeping on your left side is its positive impact on digestion. The digestive system is a complex network of organs responsible for breaking down food and absorbing nutrients. When you sleep on your left side, gravity naturally facilitates the movement of food from the small intestine into the large intestine, promoting smoother digestion and regular bowel movements.

The position of the stomach and pancreas is such that they hang naturally to the left. By sleeping on your left side, you allow these organs to rest in a more anatomically neutral position, potentially reducing the risk of acid reflux and heartburn. For those prone to digestive issues, this simple change in sleep posture might be a game-changer.

18

Continuation

Cardiovascular Support: Following the Natural Flow

Your circulatory system is another beneficiary of the left-side sleeping position. The heart, a vital organ that pumps blood throughout the body, is located slightly to the left of the center. When you sleep on your left side, you enable gravity to promote the natural flow of blood and lymphatic fluid.

The inferior vena cava, a large vein that carries deoxygenated blood from the lower half of the body to the heart, is on the right side. By sleeping on the left, you prevent compression of this vein, ensuring a smoother return of blood to the heart. This may contribute to reduced strain on the heart and better circulation overall.

The Respiratory Advantage: Easing Breathing Woes

Do you often find yourself waking up feeling congested or struggling with snoring? The position you sleep in can influence your respiratory system, and the left side has some notable advantages.

The right lung is larger than the left, consisting of three lobes compared to the left lung's two. Sleeping on your left side allows the right lung more room to expand, potentially enhancing oxygen intake. Moreover, this position can help reduce the pressure on the heart and facilitate smoother breathing, making it a valuable practice for those with respiratory conditions or anyone aiming for a more refreshing night's sleep.

19

Continuation

Pregnancy and Left-Side Sleeping: A Win-Win Situation

For expectant mothers, sleeping on the left side is often recommended by healthcare professionals. This position improves blood flow to the uterus, kidneys, and fetus. It helps prevent the uterus from pressing against the liver, ensuring optimal circulation. Pregnant women who adopt the left-side sleeping position may experience better nutrient absorption, reduced swelling, and enhanced overall comfort during sleep.

Addressing Snoring and Sleep Apnea: A Natural Remedy?

Snoring and sleep apnea can significantly impact the quality of your sleep and that of your sleep partner. While many factors contribute to these issues, sleep position is one element that might make a difference. Sleeping on your left side may help keep the airways more open, reducing the likelihood of snoring and potentially alleviating mild sleep apnea symptoms.

Enhancing Brain Health: The Glymphatic System Connection

The glymphatic system, a recently discovered waste clearance system in the brain, plays a crucial role in removing toxins and waste products. Studies suggest that the glymphatic system is more active during sleep, particularly during the deep, restorative stages. Sleeping on your left side might facilitate the optimal function of this system, potentially supporting brain health by promoting the efficient elimination of waste.

20

Sleeping Posture

ow to Make the Transition to Left-Side Sleeping

While the benefits of left-side sleeping are compelling, changing your sleep position can be challenging, especially if you're accustomed to another posture. Here are some tips to make the transition smoother:

1. Gradual Adjustment:

If you usually sleep on your back or right side, transitioning directly to the left side might be uncomfortable. Start by incorporating short periods of left-side sleeping and gradually increase the duration.

2. Use Pillows for Support:

Place a pillow between your legs and another to support your back. This can help align your spine and make left-side sleeping more comfortable.

3. Create a Relaxing Bedtime Routine:

Engage in calming activities before bed to promote relaxation. This can make it easier to adopt a new sleep position.

4. Invest in a Comfortable Mattress and Pillows:

The right mattress and pillows can make a significant difference in your comfort level and sleep quality.

5. Consult a Healthcare Professional:

If you have existing health conditions or concerns, consult with a healthcare professional before making significant changes to your sleep habits.

Conclusion: A Small Change with Big Benefits

In the pursuit of a healthier lifestyle, we often underestimate the impact of simple habits. Sleeping on your left side is one such small change that can yield substantial benefits for your digestive system, cardiovascular health, respiratory function, and overall well-being. While individual preferences and health conditions vary, experimenting with different sleep positions and finding what works best for you is a valuable journey toward better sleep and improved health. So, the next time you find yourself settling into bed, consider giving the left side a try—your body might just thank you for it.

21

The Transformative Power of Deep Breathing: A Holistic Approach to Digestion and Well-Being

In the hustle and bustle of our daily lives, taking a moment to breathe deeply might seem like a small and insignificant act. However, beneath the surface of our conscious awareness, the simple act of deep breathing can unfold a cascade of benefits, especially when it comes to digestion and overall health. Let's embark on a journey to explore the profound connection between our breath, digestion, and well-being.

Understanding the Basics: Breath and the Autonomic Nervous System

To comprehend the impact of deep breathing on digestion, it's crucial to understand the autonomic nervous system (ANS). The ANS is like the autopilot system of our body, regulating functions such as heart rate, respiratory rate, and digestion without our conscious effort. It has two main branches: the sympathetic nervous system (SNS), often associated with the "fight or flight" response, and the parasympathetic nervous system (PNS), known as the "rest and digest" system.

42

Deep breathing acts as a switch, allowing us to consciously influence the balance between the sympathetic and parasympathetic systems. When we engage in slow, deep breaths, we activate the PNS, promoting a state of relaxation and optimal conditions for digestion.

22

Gut and Brain

T*he Gut-Brain Connection: Breath as a Bridge*

The gut and the brain are intricately connected, forming what is often referred to as the gut-brain axis. This bidirectional communication system allows for constant information exchange between the central nervous system and the enteric nervous system, which is embedded in the lining of the gastrointestinal tract.

Stress, a common companion in our fast-paced lives, can negatively impact digestion. When we're stressed, the SNS takes precedence, diverting resources away from digestion and towards the perceived "fight or flight" situation. This can lead to a range of digestive issues, from indigestion to irritable bowel syndrome (IBS). Deep breathing, acting as a bridge between the gut and the brain, helps signal to the body that it's time to rest and digest, countering the negative effects of stress on our digestive processes.

23

Digestive Fuel

Deep breathing serves as a powerful tool to increase oxygenation throughout the body, including the digestive organs. Oxygen is essential for the energy-intensive process of breaking down food into nutrients that our body can absorb. By consciously taking in more oxygen through deep breaths, we provide a robust fuel source for the digestive system, enhancing its efficiency.

Furthermore, increased oxygenation supports the growth of beneficial bacteria in the gut. These microorganisms play a crucial role in maintaining a healthy balance in the digestive tract, influencing everything from nutrient absorption to immune function. A well-oxygenated system creates an environment conducive to the flourishing of these beneficial bacteria.

24

Breathing Techniques

tress Reduction and Inflammation: A Breath of Fresh Air

Chronic stress is closely linked to inflammation, a common denominator in various chronic diseases, including those affecting the digestive system. The anti-inflammatory effects of deep breathing can be profound. By activating the PNS, deep breathing helps dampen the body's inflammatory response, mitigating the risk of inflammation-related digestive issues such as inflammatory bowel disease (IBD) and acid reflux.

Moreover, reducing stress through deep breathing positively impacts the gut's permeability. Chronic stress can compromise the integrity of the intestinal barrier, leading to a condition known as "leaky gut." This increased permeability allows substances to leak into the bloodstream, triggering inflammation and potentially contributing to a host of digestive problems. Deep breathing, as a stress-reduction tool, acts as a protective shield, helping to maintain the integrity of the gut barrier.

46

25

Mindful Eating

indful Eating: Savoring Each Breath and Bite

The benefits of deep breathing extend beyond the act itself; they seamlessly integrate into the realm of mindful eating. Mindful eating involves paying full attention to the sensory experience of eating, from the taste and texture of the food to the act of chewing and swallowing. Deep breathing aligns perfectly with this practice.

Before a meal, taking a few deep breaths can transition the body into a state conducive to optimal digestion. It allows us to disengage from the stressors of the day and be present in the moment. As we eat, continuing to incorporate deep, intentional breaths can slow down the pace of our eating, preventing overeating and promoting better digestion. The act of mindful breathing in tandem with eating creates a harmonious symphony, enhancing the overall experience and benefits of both practices.

Practical Tips: Incorporating Deep Breathing into Daily Life

Now that we understand the profound impact of deep breathing on digestion and overall health, the question arises: How can we seamlessly integrate this practice into our daily lives? Here are some practical tips:

1. Morning Ritual:

Begin your day with a few minutes of deep breathing. This sets a positive tone and primes your body for the day ahead.

2. Before Meals:

Take a moment to breathe deeply before each meal. This not only prepares your body for digestion but also cultivates a mindful eating habit.

3. Midday Reset:

When stress starts to creep in during the day, take a short break for deep breathing. This can be particularly beneficial in high-stakes or pressure-filled environments.

4. Evening Wind-Down:

As part of your evening routine, engage in deep breathing to signal to your body that it's time to relax and transition into restful sleep.

5. Incorporate Mindfulness:

Combine deep breathing with mindfulness practices. Whether it's a brief meditation session or simply being fully present in the current moment, mindfulness amplifies the benefits of deep breathing.

In conclusion, the art of deep breathing goes far beyond a mere relaxation technique; it's a gateway to holistic well-being. By influencing the autonomic nervous system, oxygenating the body, reducing stress, and fostering mindful eating, deep breathing becomes a cornerstone for digestive health. In a world that often encourages us to rush through life, taking the time to breathe deeply is a simple yet transformative act—one that nourishes not just the body, but the mind and spirit as well. So, take a deep breath, and let the journey to better digestion and overall health begin.

27

The Transformative Power of Water: A Holistic Approach to Overall Health

In the pursuit of a healthier and more fulfilling life, we often seek complex solutions, forgetting the simple yet profound impact that the basics can have on our well-being. Water, the elixir of life, plays a pivotal role in our existence, and a mindful approach to its consumption can lead to transformative effects on our overall health.

Understanding the Essence of Water:

Before delving into the water affirmation technique, let's remind ourselves of the fundamental role water plays in our bodies. Up to 60% of the human adult body is water, and it's involved in practically every bodily function. From aiding digestion to regulating temperature and transporting nutrients, the importance of water cannot be overstated.

The Water Affirmation Technique Unveiled

The water affirmation technique is a simple yet potent practice that involves infusing your daily water intake with positive affirmations. Affirmations are positive statements that, when repeated consistently, can influence your thoughts, behaviors, and even your health. When combined with the act of hydration, they create a powerful synergy that contributes to overall well-being.

28

Water Affirmation Techniques

S*teps to Embrace the Water Affirmation Technique:*

1. Conscious Hydration:

Begin by making your hydration a conscious act. Often, we drink water mindlessly, not fully appreciating its significance. Pause for a moment before taking a sip, acknowledging that you are nourishing your body and revitalizing your spirit.

2. Choose Affirmations:

Select affirmations that resonate with you and align with your health goals. These could range from simple statements like "I am vibrant and healthy" to more specific ones tailored to your needs, such as "Every drop of water I drink cleanses and rejuvenates me."

3. Infuse Intention:

As you drink water, say your chosen affirmations either silently or aloud. Imagine the water carrying the positive energy of your affirmations, permeating every cell of your body. Visualization enhances the impact of the practice.

4. Consistency is Key:

Like any habit, the effectiveness of the water affirmation technique lies in consistency. Incorporate it into your daily routine, perhaps starting your day with a glass of positively charged water, or integrating it into regular breaks.

29

Continuation

T*he Mind-Body Connection:*

The water affirmation technique operates on the principle of the mind-body connection. Scientifically, the mind and body are intertwined in ways that modern medicine is continually unraveling. Positive thoughts and emotions can trigger the release of neuropeptides and endorphins, promoting physical well-being.

When you infuse your water with positive affirmations, you're not just hydrating your body but also programming your mind for health. Over time, this can lead to a more optimistic outlook, reduced stress levels, and even positive physiological changes.

Hydration and Detoxification:

Water is nature's detoxifier. It flushes out toxins, aids digestion, and supports kidney function. By coupling hydration with affirmations, you amplify the detoxifying effect. The power of positive intention combined with the physical act of cleansing creates a holistic approach to detoxification.

55

As you affirm your body's ability to eliminate waste and envision each sip purifying you, you strengthen your connection to the detoxifying process. This mental reinforcement can potentially enhance the efficiency of your body's natural detox mechanisms.

30

Emotional Nourishment

Beyond the physical benefits, the water affirmation technique addresses emotional well-being. The act of mindfulness during hydration brings attention to the present moment, a practice rooted in mindfulness and meditation traditions. This can be particularly beneficial in reducing anxiety and promoting mental clarity.

Affirmations chosen for emotional well-being further enhance the impact. For instance, affirmations like "I am calm and centered" or "My emotions flow through me, leaving me at peace" can contribute to emotional resilience.

Rituals and Routine

In a world filled with constant demands and distractions, establishing rituals that promote health is essential. The water affirmation technique can become a daily ritual, a moment of self-care that transcends the physical act of drinking water. Rituals have a grounding effect, providing a sense of stability and control amidst life's uncertainties.

Incorporating this technique into your routine transforms a mundane task into a meaningful practice. Whether it's the first glass you drink in the morning or the one you savor before bed, each instance becomes an opportunity to nurture your body and mind.

31

Continuation

T*he Ripple Effect*

The benefits of the water affirmation technique extend beyond individual well-being. As you cultivate a mindful approach to hydration, you may find that positive energy ripples into other aspects of your life. Improved mood, enhanced focus, and a general sense of well-being can positively influence your interactions with others, creating a ripple effect in your social and professional spheres.

Closing Thoughts

The water affirmation technique encapsulates the essence of holistic health—addressing not only the physical but also the mental and emotional dimensions of well-being. It's a practice that bridges the simplicity of hydration with the profound impact of positive thinking.

As you embark on this journey of conscious hydration, remember that transformation is a gradual process. The small, consistent steps you take today can lead to significant changes in your overall health tomorrow. Embrace the power of water, infuse it with positivity, and watch as this simple yet profound practice becomes a catalyst for a healthier and more vibrant life.